Practice the CFAT!

Canadian Forces Aptitude Test
Practice Test Questions

Published by

Complete **TEST** Preparation Inc.

Copyright Notice

The Canadian Armed Forces is not involved in the production of, and does not endorse this publication.

Version 7.0 February 2018

ISBN: 9781928077640

Published by
Complete Test Preparation Inc.
Victoria BC Canada

Visit us on the web at http://www.test-preparation.ca
Printed in the USA

About Complete Test Preparation Inc.

The Complete Test Preparation Team has been publishing high quality study materials since 2005. Over 1 million students from all over the world visit our websites every year, and thousands of students, teachers and parents all over the world (over 100 countries) have purchased our teaching materials, curriculum, study guides and practice tests.

Complete Test Preparation is committed to providing students with the best study materials and practice tests available on the market. Members of our team combine years of teaching experience, with experienced writers and editors, all with advanced degrees.

Feedback

We welcome your feedback. Email us at feedback@test-preparation.ca with your comments and suggestions. We carefully review all suggestions and often incorporate reader suggestions into upcoming versions. As a Print on Demand Publisher, we update our products frequently.

Find us on Facebook

Errata

Check the URL below for a list of errors and their corrections (if any) that were found after publication.

https://www.test-preparation.ca/cfat-errata/

Contents

Getting Started

CONGRATULATIONS! By deciding to take the Canadian Forces Aptitude Test (CFAT), you have taken the first step toward a great future! Of course, there is no point in taking this important examination unless you intend to do your very best to earn the highest grade you possibly can. That means getting yourself organized and discovering the best approaches, methods and strategies to master the material. Yes, that will require real effort and dedication on your part but if you are willing to focus your energy and devote the study time necessary, before you know it you will be opening that letter of acceptance to the Armed Services specialty of your dreams.

We know that taking on a new endeavour can be a little scary, and it is easy to feel unsure of where to begin. That's where we come in. This study guide is designed to help you improve your test-taking skills, show you a few tricks of the trade and increase both your competency and confidence.

The Canadian Armed Forces Aptitude Test

The CFAT has 3 sections, Verbal Skills, including basic vocabulary and verbal analogies, Spatial Ability, where you are asked to recognize shapes and patterns, and Problem Solving, which includes, word problems (arithmetic reasoning), sequences and non-verbal, where you are asked to recognize shapes after some transformation, for example, rotation.

While we seek to make our guide as comprehensive as possible, note that like all entrance exams, the CFAT Exam might be adjusted at some future point. New material might be added, or content that is no longer relevant or applicable might be removed. It is always a good idea to give the materials you receive when you register to take the CFAT a careful review.

Practice Test Questions Set 1

THE PRACTICE TEST PORTION PRESENTS QUESTIONS THAT ARE REPRESENTATIVE OF THE TYPE OF QUESTION YOU SHOULD EXPECT TO FIND ON THE CFAT. The questions below are not the same as you will find on the CFAT - that would be too easy! And nobody knows what the questions will be and they change all the time. Below are general questions that cover the same areas as the CFAT. So, while the format and exact wording of the questions may differ slightly, and change from year to year, if you can answer the questions below, you will have no problem with the CFAT.

For the best results, take these practice test questions as if it were the real exam. Set aside time when you will not be disturbed, and a location that is quiet and free of distractions. Read the instructions carefully, read each question carefully, and answer to the best of your ability.

Use the bubble answer sheets provided. When you have completed the practice test questions, check your answer against the answer key and read the explanation provided.

Verbal Ability Answer Sheet

	A	B	C	D	E			A	B	C	D	E
1	○	○	○	○	○		21	○	○	○	○	○
2	○	○	○	○	○		22	○	○	○	○	○
3	○	○	○	○	○		23	○	○	○	○	○
4	○	○	○	○	○		24	○	○	○	○	○
5	○	○	○	○	○		25	○	○	○	○	○
6	○	○	○	○	○		26	○	○	○	○	○
7	○	○	○	○	○		27	○	○	○	○	○
8	○	○	○	○	○		28	○	○	○	○	○
9	○	○	○	○	○		29	○	○	○	○	○
10	○	○	○	○	○		30	○	○	○	○	○
11	○	○	○	○	○							
12	○	○	○	○	○							
13	○	○	○	○	○							
14	○	○	○	○	○							
15	○	○	○	○	○							
16	○	○	○	○	○							
17	○	○	○	○	○							
18	○	○	○	○	○							
19	○	○	○	○	○							
20	○	○	○	○	○							

Spatial Ability Answer Sheet

	A	B	C	D
1	○	○	○	○
2	○	○	○	○
3	○	○	○	○
4	○	○	○	○
5	○	○	○	○
6	○	○	○	○
7	○	○	○	○
8	○	○	○	○
9	○	○	○	○
10	○	○	○	○
11	○	○	○	○
12	○	○	○	○
13	○	○	○	○
14	○	○	○	○
15	○	○	○	○
16	○	○	○	○
17	○	○	○	○
18	○	○	○	○
19	○	○	○	○
20	○	○	○	○

Problem Solving Ability Answer Sheet

	A	B	C	D	E			A	B	C	D	E
1	○	○	○	○	○		21	○	○	○	○	○
2	○	○	○	○	○		22	○	○	○	○	○
3	○	○	○	○	○		23	○	○	○	○	○
4	○	○	○	○	○		24	○	○	○	○	○
5	○	○	○	○	○		25	○	○	○	○	○
6	○	○	○	○	○		26	○	○	○	○	○
7	○	○	○	○	○		27	○	○	○	○	○
8	○	○	○	○	○		28	○	○	○	○	○
9	○	○	○	○	○		29	○	○	○	○	○
10	○	○	○	○	○		30	○	○	○	○	○
11	○	○	○	○	○							
12	○	○	○	○	○							
13	○	○	○	○	○							
14	○	○	○	○	○							
15	○	○	○	○	○							
16	○	○	○	○	○							
17	○	○	○	○	○							
18	○	○	○	○	○							
19	○	○	○	○	○							
20	○	○	○	○	○							

1. SUCCULENT means the same as

    a. Dull
    b. Adventurous
    c. Sweet
    d. Juicy

2. CONSTRUE means the same as

    a. Decide
    b. Design
    c. Interpret
    d. Examine

3. INDUSTRIOUS means the same as

    a. Sad
    b. Hard working
    c. Loving
    d. Funny

4. HESITANT means the same as

    a. Willing
    b. Doubtful
    c. Eager
    d. Happy

5. LUCID means the same as

    a. Dark
    b. Clear
    c. Memorable
    d. Easy

6. PECULIAR means the same as

a. New

b. Strange

c. Imaginative

d. Funny

7. VIVID means the same as

a. Glamorous

b. Bountiful

c. Varied

d. Brilliant

8. SEMBLANCE means the same as

a. Personality

b. Appearance

c. Attitude

d. Ambition

9. CONFUSED is the opposite of

a. Frustrated

b. Ashamed

c. Enlightened

d. Unknown

10. LIAISE is the opposite of

a. Uncoordinated

b. Coordinate

c. Combine

d. Encourage

11. ILLICIT is the opposite of

a. Unlawful

b. Legal

c. Anonymous

d. Deceitful

12. STERILE is the opposite of

a. Dirty

b. Alcoholic

c. Drunk

d. Drug

13. MYRIAD is the opposite of

a. Many

b. Abundant

c. Few

d. Plenty

14. PESSIMISTIC is the opposite of

a. Optimistic

b. Jovial

c. Joyful

d. Deliberate

15. PLACID is the opposite of

a. Chaotic

b. Confusing

c. Peaceful

d. Silent

16. STURDY is the opposite of

a. Strong

b. Kind

c. Rough

d. Flimsy

17. IMPORTUNE means

a. To find an opportunity

b. To ask all the time.

c. Cannot find an opportunity

d. None of the above

18. VOLATILE means

a. Not explosive

b. Catches fire easily

c. Does not catch fire

d. Explosive

19. PLAINTIVE means

a. Happy

b. Mournful

c. Faint

d. Plain

20. NEXUS means

a. A connection

b. A telephone switch

c. Part of a computer

d. None of the above

21. INHERENT means

  a. To receive money in a will
  b. An essential part of
  c. To receive money from a will
  d. None of the above

22. TORPID means

  a. Fast
  b. Rapid
  c. Sluggish
  d. Violent

23. GREGARIOUS means

  a. Sociable
  b. Introverted
  c. Large
  d. Solitary

24. NEST is to BIRD as CAVE is to

  a. Bear
  b. Petal
  c. House
  d. Dog

25. TEACHER is to SCHOOL as WAITRESS is to

  a. Office
  b. Coffee shop
  c. Customer
  d. Student

26. PEBBLE is to BOULDER as POND is to

    a. Ocean

    b. River

    c. Drop

    d. Rapids

27. DOG is to POODLE as SHARK is to

    a. Great white

    b. Dolphin

    c. Whale

    d. Fish

28. FOX is to CHICKEN as CAT is to

    a. Rabbit

    b. Mouse

    c. Cat

    d. Hen

29. LAWYER is to TRIAL as DOCTOR is to

    a. Patient

    b. Businessman

    c. Operation

    d. Nurse

30. EAT is to FAT as BREATHE is to

    a. Inhale

    b. Live

    c. Drink

    d. Talk

Part II - Spatial Ability

1. When folded, which shape is possible?

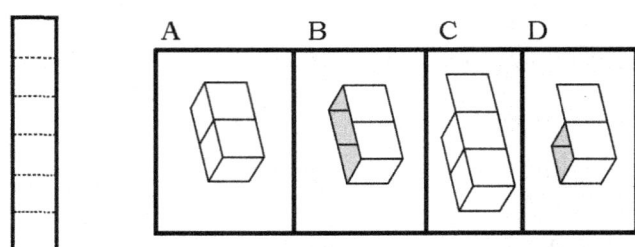

2. When folded, what pattern is possible?

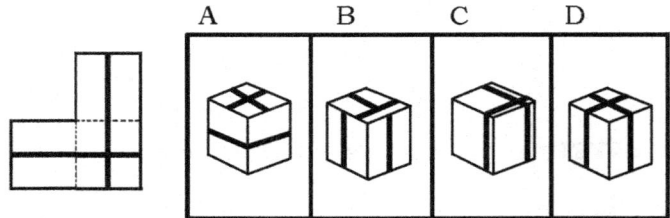

3. When folded into a loop, what will the strip of paper look like?

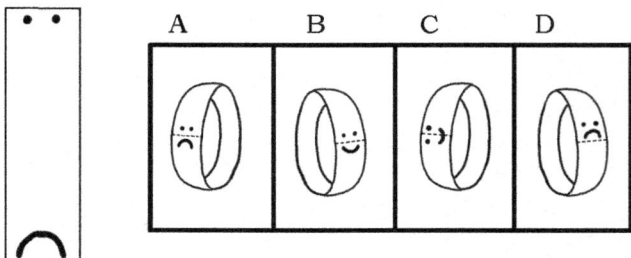

4. Which of the choices is the same pattern at a different angle?

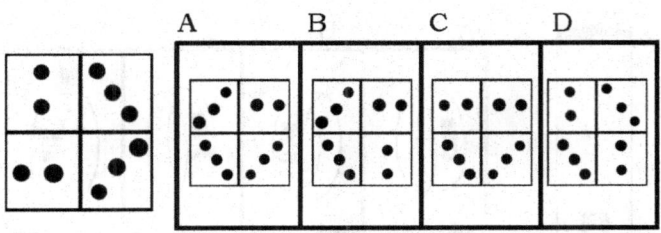

5.   When folded along the dotted lines, which shape will you get?

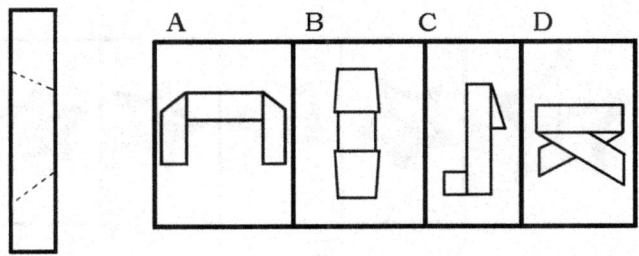

6. When folded, what pattern is possible?

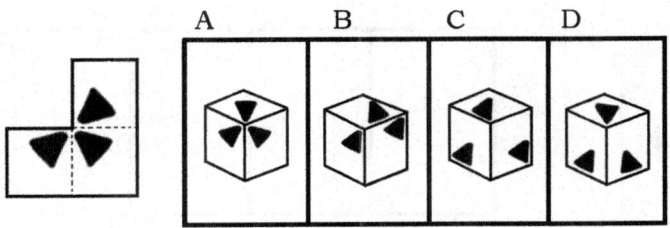

7. When folded into a loop, what will the strip of paper look like?

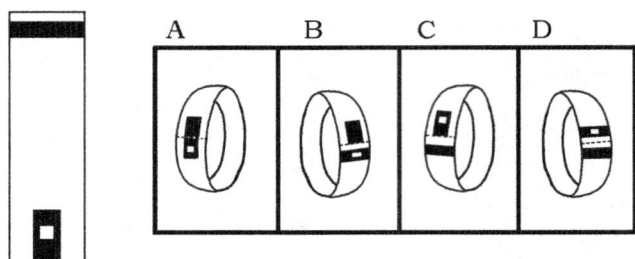

8. Which of the choices is the same pattern at a different angle?

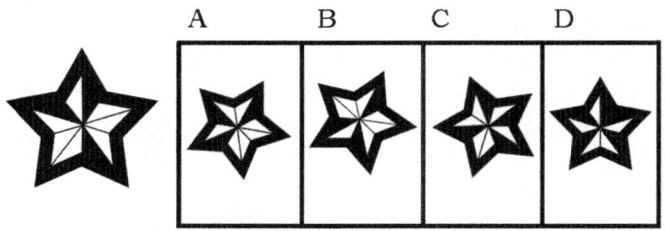

9. When folded along the dotted line, which shape will you get?

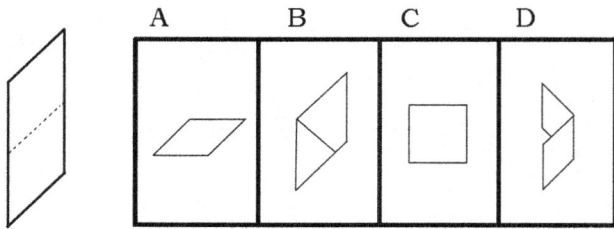

10. When folded, what pattern is possible?

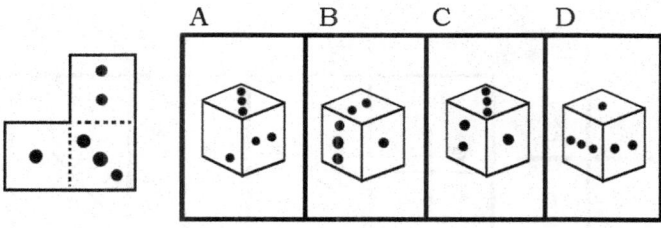

11. When folded, what pattern is possible?

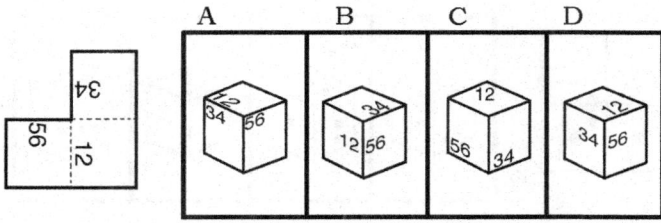

12. When folded into a loop, what will the strip of paper look like?

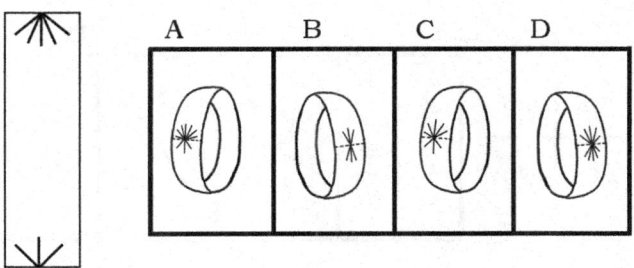

13. Which of the choices is the same pattern at a different angle?

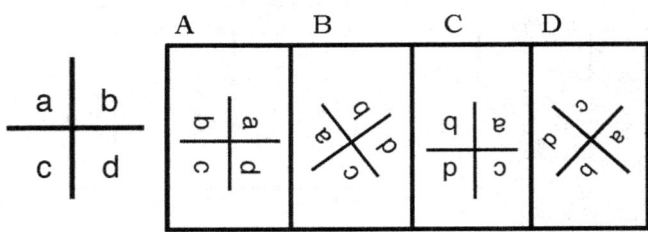

14. When folded, what pattern is possible?

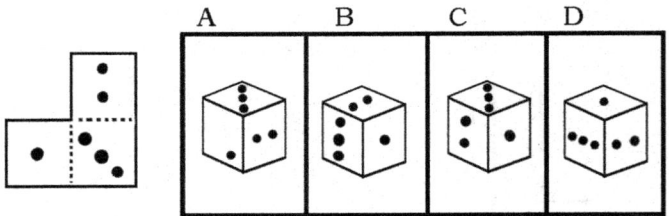

15. Which of the choices is the same pattern at a different angle?

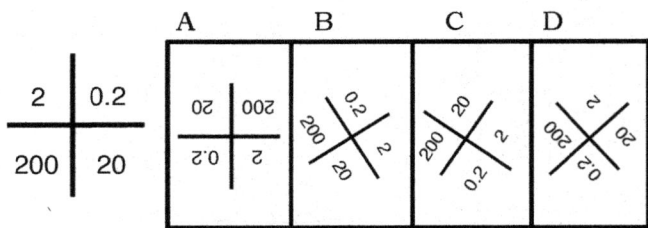

Part III - Problem Solving

**1. Consider the following sequence: 25, 33, 41, 49, ...
What number should come next?**

    a. 51

    b. 55

    c. 59

    d. 57

**2. Consider the following sequence: 6, 11, 18, 27, ...
What number should come next?**

    a. 38

    b. 35

    c. 29

    d. 30

3. Consider Box A and the relationship to the numbers in Box B. What is the missing number in Box B?

Box A

6	3
9	5

Box B

36	?
81	25

    a. 49

    b. 51

    c. 9

    d. 12

**4. Consider the following sequence: 13, 26, 52, 104, ...
What number should come next?**

      a. 208

      b. 106

      c. 200

      d. 400

**5. Consider the following sequence: 32, 26, 20, 14, ...
What number should come next?**

      a. 12

      b. 19

      c. 10

      d. 8

**6. Consider the following sequence: 12, 4, 16, ..., 36.
What is the missing number?**

      a. 18

      b. 22

      c. 20

      d. 30

**7. Consider the following sequence: 3, 9, 27, ..., 243.
What is the missing number?**

      a. 30

      b. 39

      c. 18

      d. 81

**8. Consider the following sequence: 6, 12, 24, 48, ...
What number should come next?**

    a. 48

    b. 64

    c. 60

    d. 96

**9. Consider the following sequence: 5, 6, 11, 17, ...
What number should come next?**

    a. 28

    b. 34

    c. 36

    d. 27

**10. Consider the following sequence: 26, 21, ..., 11, 6.
What is the missing number?**

    a. 27

    b. 23

    c. 16

    d. 29

11. There are 15 yellow and 35 orange balls in a basket. How many more yellow balls must be added to make the yellow balls 65%?

    a. 50

    b. 35

    c. 65

    d. 70

12. The length of a rectangle is twice its width and its area is equal to the area of a square with 12 cm. sides. What will be the perimeter of the rectangle to the nearest whole number?

    a. 51 cm.

    b. 36 cm.

    c. 46 cm.

    d. 56 cm.

13. A distributor purchased 550 kilograms of potatoes for $165. He distributed these at a rate of $6.4 per 20 kilograms to 15 shops, $3.4 per 10 kilograms to 12 shops and the remainder at $1.8 per 5 kilograms. If his total distribution cost is $10, what will his profit be?

    a. $8.60
    b. $24.60
    c. $14.90
    d. $23.40

14. 5 men have to share a load weighing 10 kg 550 g equally. How much will each man have to carry? 1 kilogram = 1000 grams.

    a. 900 g

    b. 1.5 kg

    c. 3 kg

    d. 2 kg 110 g

15. A worker's weekly salary was increased by 30%. If his new salary is $150, what was his old salary?

    a. $120

    b. $99.15

    c. $109

    d. $115.4

16. How much pay does Mr. Johnson receive if he gives half to his family, pays $250 for rent, and has exactly 3/7 of his pay left over?

    a. $3,600

    b. $2,800

    c. $1,750

    d. $3,500

17. Smith and Simon are playing a card game. Smith will win if a card drawn from a deck of 52 is either 7 or a diamond, and Simon will win if the drawn card is an even number. Which statement is more likely to be correct?

    a. Simon will win more games.

    b. Smith will win more games

    c. They have same chance of winning.

    d. A decision can not be made from the data provided.

18. Mr. White wants to tile his rectangular back yard which is 16 meters × 11 meters. The dimensions of each tile are 7 cm × 4 cm. If cost of each tile is $0.30 and 2.5% tiles break during handling. How much will it cost?

    a. $18,857

    b. $19,328

    c. $20,895

    d. $21,563

19. A map uses a scale of 1:2,000   How much distance on the ground is 5.2 inches on the map if the scale is in inches?

    a. 100,400

    b. 10, 500

    c. 10,400

    d. 10,400

20. If a train travels at 72 kilometers per hour, what distance it will cover in 12 seconds?

    a. 200 meters

    b. 220 meters

    c. 240 meters

    d. 260 meters

21. Tony bought 15 dozen eggs for $80. 16 eggs were broken during loading and unloading. The remaining he sold at $0.54 each. What will be his percentage profit? Provide answer in 2 significant digits.

    a. 11%

    b. 11.20%

    c. 11.50%

    d. 12%

22.

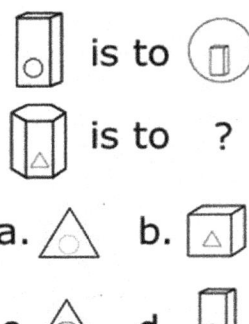

23.

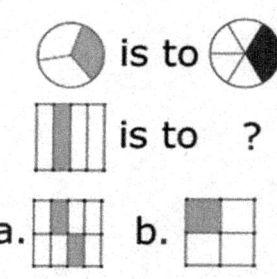

is to   ?

a. b.

c. d.

24.

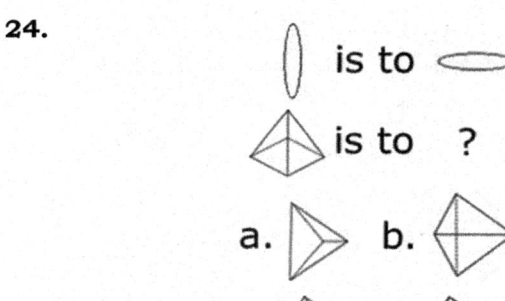

a. b.

c. d.

25.

is to

is to   ?

a. b.

c. d.

26.

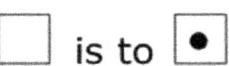 is to

is to ?

a.    b.

c.   d.

27.

is to

is to ?

a.   b.

c.   d.

28.

 is to

is to ?

a.   b.

c.   d.

29.

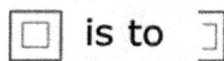 is to ⊐

⬠ is to ?

a. ⟩   b. ⟩⟩

c. ⟩   d. ⊐

30.

☐ is to ⊐

⬠ is to ?

a. ⟩   b. ⟩

c. ⟩   d. ⊐

Answer Key

1. D
Succulent means the same as juicy.

2. C
Construe means the same as interpret.

3. B
Industrious means the same as hard working.

4. B
Hesitant means the same as doubtful.

5. B
Lucid means the same as clear.

6. B
Peculiar means the same as strange.

7. D
Vivid means the same as brilliant.

8. B
Semblance means the same as appearance.

9. C
Confused is the opposite of enlightened.

10. A
Liaise is the opposite of uncoordinated.

11. B
Illicit is the opposite of legal.

12. A
Sterile is the opposite of dirty.

13. C
Myriad is the opposite of few.

14. A
Pessimistic is the opposite of optimistic.

15. A
Placid is the opposite of chaotic.

16. D
Sturdy is the opposite of flimsy.

17. B
Importune: To harass with persistent requests.

18. D
Volatile: explosive; liable to change rapidly and unpredictably.

19. B
Plaintive: Sorrowful, mournful or melancholic.

20. A
Nexus: A form of connection.

21. B
Inherent: Naturally a part or consequence of something, an essential part of.

22. C
Torpid: Lazy, lethargic or apathetic.

23. A
Gregarious: Describing one who enjoys being in crowds and socializing.

24. A
This is a functional relationship. A bird lives in a nest, the same way that a bear lives in a cave.

25. B
This is a functional relationship. A teacher works in a school in the same way that a waitress works in a coffee shop.

26. A
This is a degree relationship. A boulder is a very large pebble - both are rocks, in the same way that an ocean is a very large pond - both are bodies of water.

27. A
This is a type relationship. A poodle is a type of dog in the same way that a great white is a type of shark.

28. B
This is a predator/prey relationship. Foxes eat chickens in the same way that cats eat mice.

29. C
This is a functional relationship. A lawyer defends a client in a trial in the same way that a doctor heals a patient in an operation.

30. B
This is a cause and effect relationship. You must eat to become fat, in the same way that you must breathe to live.

Spatial Ability

1. B

2. D

3. B

4. B

5. A

6. A

7. C

8. B

9. D

10. C

11. D

12. C

13. D

14. C

15. A

Problem Solving

1. D
The numbers increase by 8.

2. A
The interval begins with 5, and increases by 2 and is added each time.
6, [+5] 11, [+7] 18, [+9] 27 [+11] **38**

3. C
The numbers in Box B are squares of the numbers in Box A.

4. A
The number doubles each time.

5. D
The numbers decrease by 6 each time.

6. C
Each number is the sum of the previous two numbers.

7. D
The number triples each time.

8. D
The numbers doubles each time.

9. A
Each number is the sum of the previous two numbers

10. C
The numbers decrease by 5 each time.

11. A
There are 50 balls in the basket now. Let x be the number of yellow balls that are to be added to make yellow balls 65%. The equation becomes $((X + 15)/X)] + 50 = 65/100$. X = 50.

12. A
Area of the square = $12 \times 12 = 144$ cm^2. Let x be the width

so 2x will be the length of rectangle. The area will be $2x^2$ and the perimeter will be 2(2x + x) = 6x. According to the condition $2x^2$ = 144 then x = 8.48cm. The perimeter will be 6 × 8.48 = 50.88 = 51 cm.

13. A

The distribution is done in three different rates and amounts:

$6.4 per 20 kilograms to 15 shops ... 20•15 = 300 kilograms distributed

$3.4 per 10 kilograms to 12 shops ... 10•12 = 120 kilograms distributed

550 - (300 + 120) = 550 - 420 = 130 kilograms left. This amount is distributed by 5 kilogram portions. So, this means that there are 130/5 = 26 shops.

$1.8 per 130 kilograms.

We need to find the amount he earned overall these distributions.

$6.4 per 20 kilograms : 6.4 * 15 = $96 for 300 kilograms

$3.4 per 10 kilograms : 3.4 * 12 = $40.8 for 120 kilograms

$1.8 per 5 kilograms : 1.8 * 26 = $46.8 for 130 kilograms

So, he earned 96 + 40.8 + 46.8 = $ 183.6

The total distribution cost is given as $10

The profit is found by: Money earned - money spent ... It is important to remember that he bought 550 kilograms of potatoes for $165 at the beginning:

Profit = 183.6 - 10 - 165 = $8.6

14. D

First, we need to convert all units to grams. Since 1000 g = 1 kg:

10 kg 550 g = 10 * 1000 g + 550 g = 10,000 g + 550 g = 10,550 g.

10,550 g is shared between 5 men. So each man will have to carry 10,550/5 = 2,110 g

2,110 g = 2,000 g + 110 g = 2 kg 110 g

15. D
Let old salary = X, therefore $150 = x + 0.30x, 150 = 1x + 0.30x, 150 = 1.30x, x = 150/1.30 =115.3846 = 115.38 = 115.4

16. D
We check the fractions taking place in the question. We see that there is a "half" (that is 1/2) and 3/7. So, we multiply the denominators of these fractions to decide how to name the total money. We say that Mr. Johnson has 14x at the beginning; he gives half of this, meaning 7x, to his family. $250 to his landlord. He has 3/7 of his money left. 3/7 of 14x is equal to:

14x * (3/7) = 6x

So,

Spent money is: 7x + 250

Unspent money is: 6x

Total money is: 14x

We write an equation: total money = spent money + unspent money

14x = 7x + 250 + 6x

14x - 7x - 6x = 250

x = 250

We are asked to find the total money that is 14x:

14x = 14 * 250 = $3500

17. A
There are 52 cards in total. Smith has 16 cards in which

he can win. So his winning probability in a single game will be 16/52. Simon has 20 cards where he will win, so his probability of a win in a single draw is 20/52. Simon has a greater chance of winning.

18. B

The area of each tile is 7 cm. X 4 cm. = 28 cm^2. The area of the yard is 16 m X 11 m = 176 m^2 = 1760000 cm^2. The number of tiles required is 1760000/28 = 62857. 2.5% of the tiles break during handling, so 1.025 X 62857 = 64429. Total cost will be 64429 X 0.3 = \$19,328.

19. C

1 inch on map = 2,000 inches on ground. So, 5.2 inches on map = 5.2•2,000 = 10,400 inches on ground.

20. C

1 hour is equal to 3,600 seconds and 1 kilometer is equal to 1000 meters.

Since this train travels 72 kilometers per hour, this means that it covers 72,000 meters in 3,600 seconds.

If it travels 72,000 meters in 3,600 seconds

It travels x meters in 12 seconds

By cross multiplication: x = 72,000 * 12 / 3,600

x = 240 meters

21. A

Let us first mention the money Tony spent: \$80

Now we need to find the money Tony earned:

He had 15 dozen eggs = 15 * 12 = 180 eggs. 16 eggs were broken. So,

Remaining number of eggs that Tony sold = 180 − 16 = 164.

Total amount he earned for selling 164 eggs = 164•0.54 = \$88.56.

As a summary, he spent \$80 and earned \$88.56.

The profit is the difference: 88.56 - 80 = $8.56

Percent profit is found by proportioning the profit to the money he spent:

(8.56 * 100)/80 = 10.7%

Checking the answers, we round 10.7 to the nearest whole number: 11%

22. C
The inside and larger shapes are reversed.

23. D
The shaded area is divided in half in the second figure.

24. D
The relation is the same figure rotated to the right.

25. B
The relation is the number of dots in the first figure is one-half the number of sides in the second figure.

26. C
The pattern is the same figure with a dot inside.

27. A
The relation is the same figure smaller, plus another figure with one more side.

28. B
The relation is the bottom half of the 3-dimensional figure.

29. C
The relation is the right half of the first object.

30. B
The relation is the right half of the first object.

Practice Test Questions Set 2

THE PRACTICE TEST PORTION PRESENTS QUESTIONS THAT ARE REPRESENTATIVE OF THE TYPE OF QUESTION YOU SHOULD EXPECT TO FIND ON THE CFAT. The questions below are not the same as you will find on the CFAT - that would be too easy! And nobody knows what the questions will be and they change all the time. Below are general questions that cover the same areas as the CFAT. So, while the format and exact wording of the questions may differ slightly, and change from year to year, if you can answer the questions below, you will have no problem with the CFAT.

For the best results, take these practice test questions as if it were the real exam. Set aside time when you will not be disturbed, and a location that is quiet and free of distractions. Read the instructions carefully, read each question carefully, and answer to the best of your ability.

Use the bubble answer sheets provided. When you have completed the practice test questions, check your answer against the answer key and read the explanation provided.

Verbal Ability Answer Sheet

	A	B	C	D	E			A	B	C	D	E
1	○	○	○	○	○		21	○	○	○	○	○
2	○	○	○	○	○		22	○	○	○	○	○
3	○	○	○	○	○		23	○	○	○	○	○
4	○	○	○	○	○		24	○	○	○	○	○
5	○	○	○	○	○		25	○	○	○	○	○
6	○	○	○	○	○		26	○	○	○	○	○
7	○	○	○	○	○		27	○	○	○	○	○
8	○	○	○	○	○		28	○	○	○	○	○
9	○	○	○	○	○		29	○	○	○	○	○
10	○	○	○	○	○		30	○	○	○	○	○
11	○	○	○	○	○							
12	○	○	○	○	○							
13	○	○	○	○	○							
14	○	○	○	○	○							
15	○	○	○	○	○							
16	○	○	○	○	○							
17	○	○	○	○	○							
18	○	○	○	○	○							
19	○	○	○	○	○							
20	○	○	○	○	○							

Spatial Ability Answer Sheet

	A	B	C	D
1	○	○	○	○
2	○	○	○	○
3	○	○	○	○
4	○	○	○	○
5	○	○	○	○
6	○	○	○	○
7	○	○	○	○
8	○	○	○	○
9	○	○	○	○
10	○	○	○	○
11	○	○	○	○
12	○	○	○	○
13	○	○	○	○
14	○	○	○	○
15	○	○	○	○
16	○	○	○	○
17	○	○	○	○
18	○	○	○	○
19	○	○	○	○
20	○	○	○	○

Problem Solving Ability Answer Sheet

	A	B	C	D	E			A	B	C	D	E
1	○	○	○	○	○		21	○	○	○	○	○
2	○	○	○	○	○		22	○	○	○	○	○
3	○	○	○	○	○		23	○	○	○	○	○
4	○	○	○	○	○		24	○	○	○	○	○
5	○	○	○	○	○		25	○	○	○	○	○
6	○	○	○	○	○		26	○	○	○	○	○
7	○	○	○	○	○		27	○	○	○	○	○
8	○	○	○	○	○		28	○	○	○	○	○
9	○	○	○	○	○		29	○	○	○	○	○
10	○	○	○	○	○		30	○	○	○	○	○
11	○	○	○	○	○							
12	○	○	○	○	○							
13	○	○	○	○	○							
14	○	○	○	○	○							
15	○	○	○	○	○							
16	○	○	○	○	○							
17	○	○	○	○	○							
18	○	○	○	○	○							
19	○	○	○	○	○							
20	○	○	○	○	○							

Part I - Verbal Skills

1. JARGON means the same as

    a. Slang
    b. Slander
    c. Plagiarism
    d. Outdated

2. RENDER means the same as

    a. Give
    b. Recognize
    c. Stem
    d. Adjust

3. INTRUSIVE means the same as

    a. Private
    b. Invasive
    c. Mysterious
    d. Unique

4. RENOWN means the same as

    a. Popular
    b. Safe
    c. Shy
    d. Curtail

5. INCOHERENT means the same as

    a. Ambiguous

    b. Lighthearted

    c. Jumbled

    d. Malignant

6. CONGENIAL means the same as

    a. Pleasant

    b. Distort

    c. Valuable

    d. Liability

7. BERATE means the same as

    a. Criticize

    b. Unspoken

    c. Tenet

    d. Turf

8. SATE means the same as

    a. Inadequate

    b. Satisfy

    c. Lacking

    d. Spectator

9. ABUNDANT is the opposite of

    a. Scarce

    b. Plenty

    c. Analysis

    d. Obtrusive

10. TOUGH is the opposite of

a. Bully
b. Gregarious
c. Weak
d. Massive

11. SIMPLE is the opposite of

a. Complex
b. Plain
c. Shy
d. Vibrant

12. EXHIBIT is the opposite of

a. Elevate
b. Conceal
c. Brood
d. Contest

13. STINGY is the opposite of

a. Tight
b. Offensive
c. Mean
d. Generous

14. ADVANCE is the opposite of

a. New
b. Retreat
c. Next
d. Followed

15. CEASE is the opposite of

a. Halt

b. Amidst

c. Delay

d. Begin

16. IMMENSE is the opposite of

a. Scary

b. Honor

c. Tiny

d. Loud

17. REDUNDANT means

a. Backup

b. Necessary repetition

c. Unnecessary repetition

d. No repetition

18. BICKER means

a. Chat

b. Discuss

c. Argue

d. Debate

19. SOMBRE means

a. Gothic

b. Black

c. Gloomy

d. Evil

20. MAVERICK means

a. Rebel

b. Conformist

c. Unconventional

d. Conventional

21. TENUOUS means

a. Strong

b. Tense

c. Firm

d. Weak

22. Pandemonium means

a. Chaos

b. Orderly

c. Quiet

d. Noisy

23. Perpetual means

a. Continuous

b. Slowly

c. Over a very long time

d. Motion

24. MELT is to LIQUID as FREEZE is to

a. Ice

b. Condense

c. Solid

d. Steam

25. CLOCK is to TIME as THERMOMETER is to

    a. Heat

    b. Radiation

    c. Energy

    d. Temperature

26. CAR is to GARAGE as PLANE is to

    a. Depot

    b. Port

    c. Hanger

    d. Harbour

27. ACTING is to THEATER as GAMBLING is to

    a. Gym

    b. Bar

    c. Club

    d. Casino

28. PORK is to PIG as BEEF is to

    a. Herd

    b. Farmer

    c. Cow

    d. Lamb

29. FRUIT is to BANANA as MAMMAL is to

    a. Rabbit

    b. Snake

    c. Fish

    d. Sparrow

30. SLUMBER is to SLEEP as BOG is to

    a. Dream

    b. Foray

    c. Swamp

    d. Night

Part II Spatial Ability

1. When folded along the dotted lines, which shape will you get?

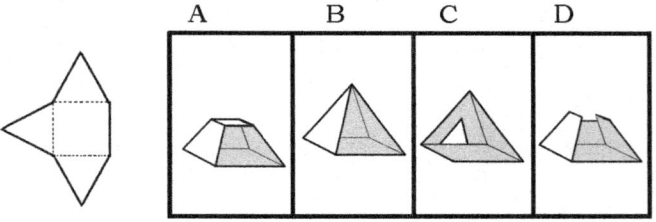

2. When folded, what pattern is possible?

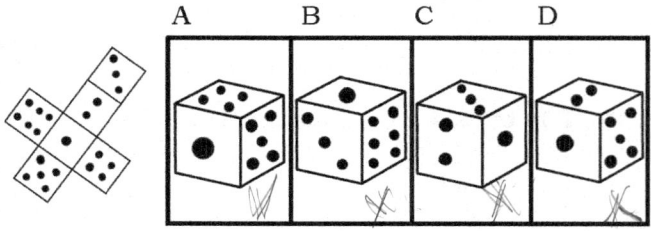

3. When folded into a loop, what will the strip of paper look like?

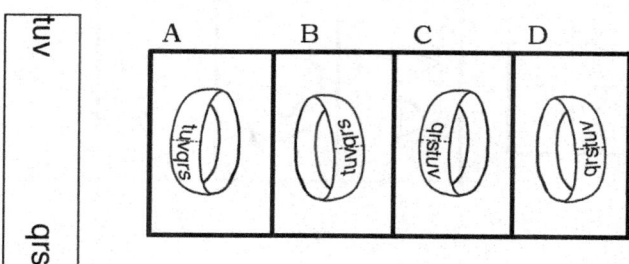

4. Which of the choices is the same pattern at a different angle?

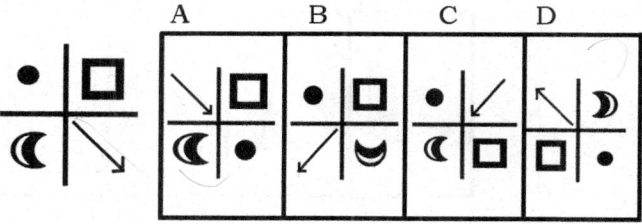

5. When put together, what 3-dimensional shape will you get?

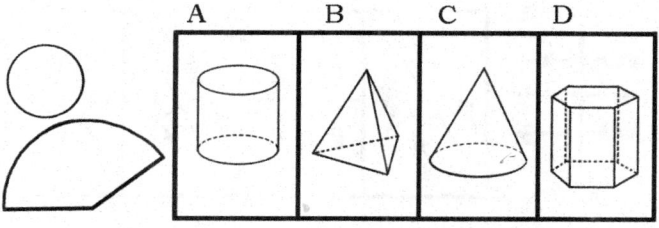

6. When folded, what pattern is possible?

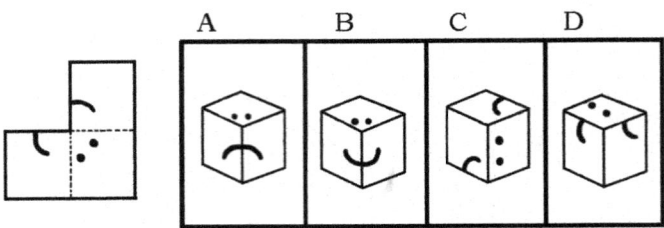

7. When folded, what pattern is possible?

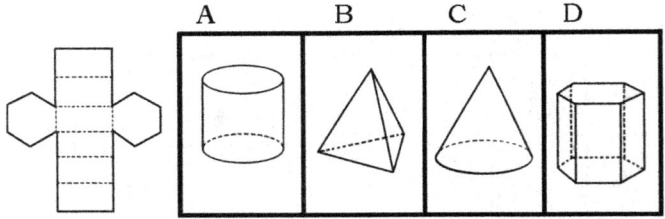

8. Which of the choices is the same pattern at a different angle?

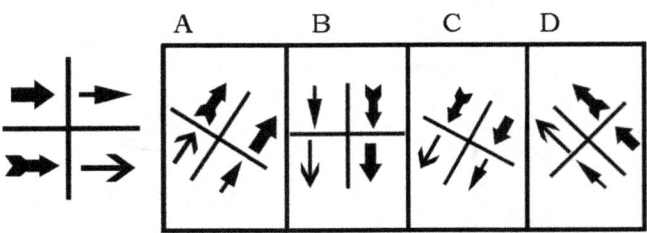

9. When put together, what 3-dimensional shape will you get?

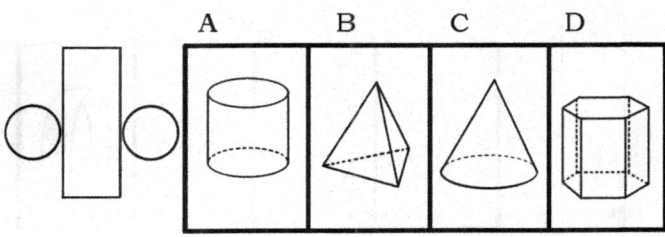

10. When folded into a loop, what will the strip of paper look like?

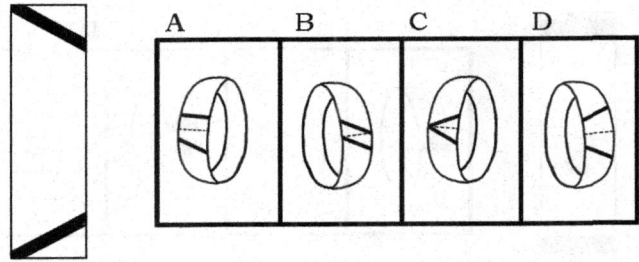

11. Which of the choices is the same pattern at a different angle?

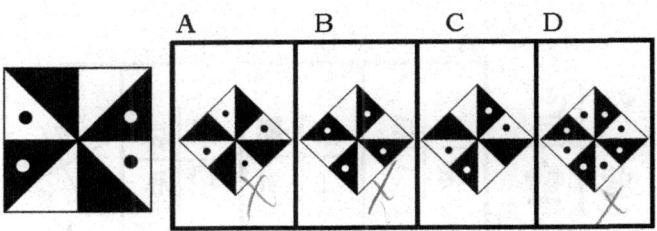

12. When put together, what 3-dimensional shape will you get?

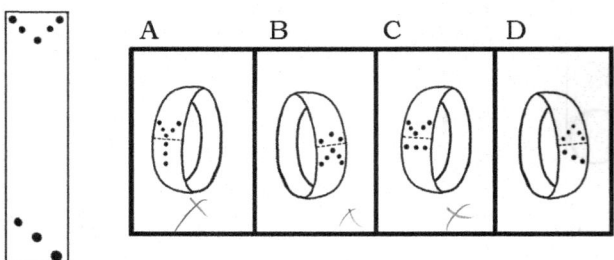

13. When folded into a loop, what will the strip of paper look like?

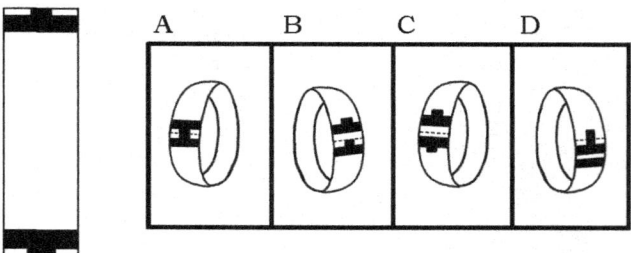

14. Which of the choices is the same pattern at a different angle?

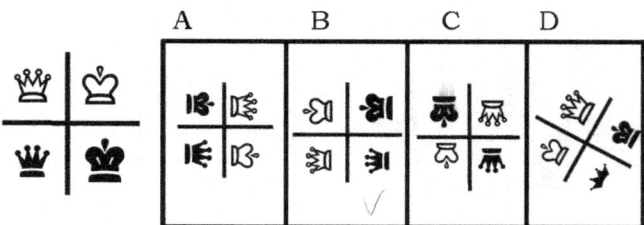

15. When folded into a loop, what will the strip of paper look like?

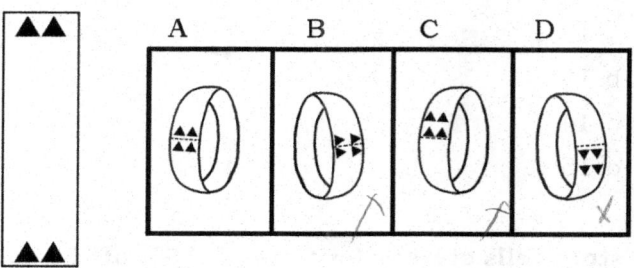

Part III - Problem Solving

1. A box is 15 cm long, 20 cm wide and 10 cm high. What is the volume of the box?

    a. 45 cm³

    b. 3,000 cm³

    c. 1500 cm³

    d. 300 cm³

2. Sarah weighs 25 pounds more than Tony. If together they weigh 205 pounds, what is Sarah's approximate weight in kilograms? Assume 1 pound = 0.4535 kilograms.

    a. 52

    b. 50

    c. 48

    d. 41

3. In a class of 83 students, 72 are present. What percent of student are absent? Provide answer up to two significant digits.

    a. 12

    b. 13

    c. 14

    d. 15

4. A store sells stereos for $545. If 15% of the cost was added to the price as value added tax, what was the cost before the tax?

    a. $490.40

    b. $473.90

    c. $575.00

    d. $593.15

5. Mr. Jones runs a factory. His total assets are $256,800 which consists of a building worth $80,500, machinery worth $125.000 and $51,300 cash. After one year what will be the total value of his assets if he has additional cash of $75,600 and the value of his building has increased by 10% per year, and his machinery depreciated by 20%?

    a. $243,450

    b. $252,450

    c. $315,450

    d. $272,350

6. Martin earns $25,000 basic pay, pays $500 rent and $860 medical allowance. He spends 40% of his total earning on food and clothing, 10% on children's education and pays $800 for utility bills. What percentage of his earning he is saving?

    a. 44%

    b. 47%

    c. 50%

    d. 54%

7. Prize money of $1,050 is to be shared among top three contestants in ratio of 7:5:3 as 1st 2nd and 3rd prizes respectively. How much more money will the 1st prize contestant get than the 3rd prize contestant?

    a. $210

    b. $280

    c. $350

    d. $490

8. The manager of a weaving factory estimates that if 10 machines run at 100% efficiency for 8 hours, they will produce 1450 meters of cloth. Due to some technical problems, 4 machines run of 95% efficiency and the remaining 6 at 90% efficiency. How many meters of cloth will these machines produce in 8 hours?

    a. 1479 meters

    b. 1310 meters

    c. 1334 meters

    d. 1285 meters

9.

 is to

△ is to ?

a. ▽   b. ◁

c. ▷   d. 🛢

10.

△ is to ▷

🛢 is to ?

a. ▷   b. ☐

c. ⬠   d. 🛢

11.

 is to △

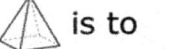 is to ?

a. △   b. ☐

c. ⬠   d. 🛢

12.

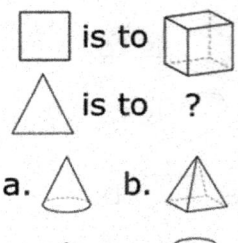

a. b.

c. d.

13.

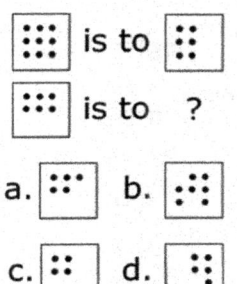

a. b.

c. d.

14.

is to

is to   ?

a. b.

c. d.

15.

⬠ is to ⬡

⬡ is to   ?

a. ☐   b. ⬡

c. ⬠   d. ⬡

16.

◯ is to ◖

▢ is to   ?

a. ▫   b. ▯

c. ▭ d. ▫

17. Consider the following sequence: ..., ..., 20, 32, 44, 56, 68. Find the first two terms.

a. -4, 8
b. 0, 12
c. -6, 8
d. 2, 8

18. Consider the following sequence: 3, 5, 10, 12, 24, ... What 2 numbers should come next?

    a. 48, 58

    b. 26, 28

    c. 48, 50

    d. 26, 52

19. Consider the following sequence: 1000, 992, 984, 976, ... What 2 numbers should come next?

    a. 968, 961

    b. 967, 960

    c. 968, 960

    d. 970, 964

20. Consider the following sequence: 0.1, 0.3, 0.9, 2.7, ... What 2 numbers should come next?

    a. -8.1, -24.3

    b. 8.1, 24.3

    c. 5.4, 10.8

    d. -5.4, -10.8

21. Consider the following sequence: 32, 16, 8, 4, ... What 3 numbers should come next?

    a. 2, 1, 0.5

    b. 2, 0, -2

    c. 0, -4, -8

    d. 2, 1, 0

22. Consider the following sequence: 3, ..., 9, 12, 15. What is the missing number?

    a. 4

    b. 7

    c. 6

    d. 5

23. Consider the following sequence: 1132, 1121, ... , 1199, ... What number comes next?

    a. 1109

    b. 1188

    c. 1189

    d. 1180

24. Consider the following sequence: 95, 90, ..., 80, 75. What is the missing number?

    a. 87

    b. 85

    c. 86

    d. 80

25. Consider the following sequence: ..., 75, 65, 60, 50, 45, 35, ... What 2 numbers are missing?

    a. 70, 35

    b. 65, 35

    c. 80, 30

    d. 65, 30

26. Consider the following sequence: 91, 85, ..., ..., 67, 61. What 2 numbers are missing?

    a. 81, 71

    b. 78, 72

    c. 80, 70

    d. 79, 73

27. Consider the following sequence: ..., ..., 120, 129, 138, 147. Find the first two terms.

    a. 102, 111

    b. 100, 110

    c. 102, 112

    d. 99, 111

28. Consider the following sequence: ..., 95, 88, 93, 86, 91, ... What 2 numbers are missing?

    a. 88,98

    b. 90, 98

    c. 100, 84

    d. 90, 84

29. Consider the following sequence: 76, 64, 54, 46, ..., 36, ..., . What 2 numbers are missing?

    a. 40,32

    b. 40, 34

    c. 42, 30

    d. 42, 32

30. Consider the following sequence: 3, ..., 12, ..., 48, 96. What 2 numbers are missing?

    a. 6, 36

    b. 6, 18

    c. 8, 16

    d. 6, 24

Answer Key

Part 1 - Verbal Skills

1. A
Jargon means the same as slang.

2. A
Render means the same as give.

3. B
Intrusive means the same as invasive.

4. A
Renown means the same as popular.

5. C
Incoherent means the same as jumbled.

6. A
Congenial means the same as pleasant.

7. A
Berate means the same as criticize.

8. B
Sate means the same as satisfy.

9. A
Abundant is the opposite of scarce.

10. C
Tough is the opposite of weak.

11. A
Simple is the opposite of complex.

12. B
Exhibit is the opposite of conceal.

13. D
Stingy is the opposite of generous.

14. B
Advance is the opposite of retreat.

15. D
Cease is the opposite of begin.

16. C
Immense is the opposite of tiny.

17. C
Redundant: Repetitive or needlessly wordy.

18. C
Bicker: To quarrel in a tiresome, insulting manner.

19. C
Sombre: Dark; gloomy.

20. A
Maverick: Showing independence in thoughts or actions, a rebel.

21. D
Tenuous: Thin in substance or consistency, weak.

22. A
Pandemonium: Chaos; tumultuous or lawless violence.

23. A
Perpetual: Continuing uninterrupted.

24. C
This is a process relationship. The first word is the process which creates the second. For example, ice melts to liquid in the same way water freezes to solid.

25. D
This is a measurement relationship. Clocks measure time in the same way thermometers measure temperature.

26. C
A car is kept in a garage the same way that a plane is kept in a hangar.

27. D
This is a place relationship. Acting is done in a theater in the same way gambling is done in a casino.

28. C
Pork is the meat of a pig in the same way beef is the meat of a cow.

29. A
This is a classification relationship.   The first is the class to which the second belongs.

Fruit -> banana
Mammal -> rabbit

30. C
Slumber is a synonym for sleep and bog is a synonym for swamp.

Spatial Ability

1. B

2. A

3. D

4. D

5. C

6. B

7. D

8. C

9. A

10. C

11. C

12. D

13. A

14. B

15. A

Problem Solving

1. B
Formula for volume of a shape is L x W x H = 15 x 20 x 10 = 3,000 cm³

2. A
Let us denote Sarah's weight by "x." Then, since she weighs 25 pounds more than Tony, he will be x - 25. They together weigh 205 pounds which means that the sum of the two representations will be equal to 205:

Sarah : x

Tony : x - 25

x + (x - 25) = 205 ... by arranging this equation we have:

x + x - 25 = 205

2x - 25 = 205 ... we add 25 to each side to have the x term alone on one side:

2x - 25 + 25 = 205 + 25

2x = 230

x = 230/2

x = 115 pounds → Sarah weighs 115 pounds. Since 1 pound is 0.4535 kilograms, we need to multiply 115 by 0.4535 to have her weight in kilograms:

x = 115 * 0.4535 = 52.1525 kilograms → this is equal to 52 when rounded to the nearest whole number.

3. B
Number of absent students = 83 – 72 = 11

Percentage of absent students is found by proportioning the number of absent students to total number of students in the class = (11 * 100)/83 = 13.25

Checking the answers, we round 13.25 to the nearest whole number: 13%

4. B
Actual cost = X, therefore, 545 = x + 0.15x, 545 = 1x +

0.15x, 545 = 1.15x,
x = 545/1.15 = $473.9

5. C
Cash = 51,300 + $75600 = $126,900. Building after one year = 80500 X 1.1 = $88550. Machinery after one year = 125000 X 0.8 = $100000. Total asset value = $315,450.

6. B
25,000 - (500 + 860) = 23640.
Food and clothing expense = 0.4 X 23640 = 9456
Education = 23640 X 0.1 = 2364
Utilities = 800
Total expenses = 9456 + 2364 + 800 = 12620.
Amount of savings 23640 - 12620 = 11020
11020/23640 = X/100
X = 1102000/23640 = 46.6% and round up to 47%.

7. B
The 1st prize winner will receive 7 X 1050/15 = $490.
The 3rd prize winner will receive, 3 X 1050/15 = $210.
The difference is 490 - 210 = $280.

8. C
At 100% efficiency 1 machine produces 1450/10 = 145 m of cloth.

At 95% efficiency, 4 machines produce 4 *145 * 95/100 = 551 m of cloth.

At 90% efficiency, 6 machines produce 6 * 145 * 90/100 = 783 m of cloth.

Total cloth produced by all 10 machines = 551 + 783 = 1334 m

Since the information provided, and the question are based on 8 hours, we did not need to use time to reach the answer.

9. A
The relation is the same figure rotated.

10. D
The relation is the same figure rotated.

11. B
The relation is a 3-dimensional figure to a 2-dimensional figure.

12. B
The relation is a 2-dimensional figure to a 3-dimensional figure.

13. C
The first figure has 9 dots in a square and the second figure has 6 dots, which is 1/3 removed.

14. C
The relation is a 3-dimensional figure to a rotated 2-dimensional figure.

15. B
The second figure contains more sides than the first.

16. B
The relation is the given figure to a horizontally compressed figure.

17. A
The sequence is increasing by 12. To find first two terms, we solve backwards by subtracting 12.

18. D
The sequence is increasing by adding 2 and multiplying 2 alternately. The next 2 terms are 24 + 2= 26 and 26 x 2 = 52.

19. C
The sequence is decreasing by 8.

20. B
The sequence is increasing by multiplying each the last term by 3. 2.7 x 3= 8.1 and 8.1 x 3 = 24.3

21. A
The sequence is decreasing by dividing the last term by 2.

22. C
The sequence is increasing by +3.

23. B
The sequence is reducing by 11.

24. B
The sequence is decreasing by +5.

25. C
The sequence is decreasing by -5 and -10 alternately; the first term is 75 – 5 = 70 and the last term is 35 – 10= 30.

26. D
The sequence is increasing by +6.

27. A
The sequence is increasing by +9.

28. D
The sequence is increasing and decreasing alternately. It increases by +5 and decreases by -7. The first term will thus be the second term 95 – 5 = 90 and the last term will be 91 – 7 = 84.

29. B
The difference between the terms starts from 12 and decreases by 2 i.e. 12, 10,8,6,4,2. The missing terms are 46 – 6=40 and 34 – 0 =34

30. D
Each term is being doubled or multiplied by 2 to get the next term. 3 x 2 = 6 and 12 x 2 = 24.

Conclusion

C ONGRATULATIONS! You have made it this far because you have applied yourself diligently to practicing for the exam and no doubt improved your potential score considerably! Getting into a good school is a huge step in a journey that might be challenging at times but will be many times more rewarding and fulfilling. That is why being prepared is so important.

Study then Practice and then Succeed!

Good Luck!

FREE Ebook Version

Download a FREE Ebook version of the publication!

Suitable for tablets, iPad, iPhone, or any smart phone.

Go to **http://tinyurl.com/nrn6krq**

Thanks!

If you enjoyed this book and would like to order additional copies for yourself or for friends, please check with your local bookstore, favourite online bookseller or visit www.test-preparation.ca and place your order directly with the publisher.

Feedback to the publisher may be sent by email to feedback@test-preparation.ca

CPSIA information can be obtained
at www.ICGtesting.com
Printed in the USA
LVOW13s1146210618
581494LV00018B/469/P